Istanbul,
Once Constantinople

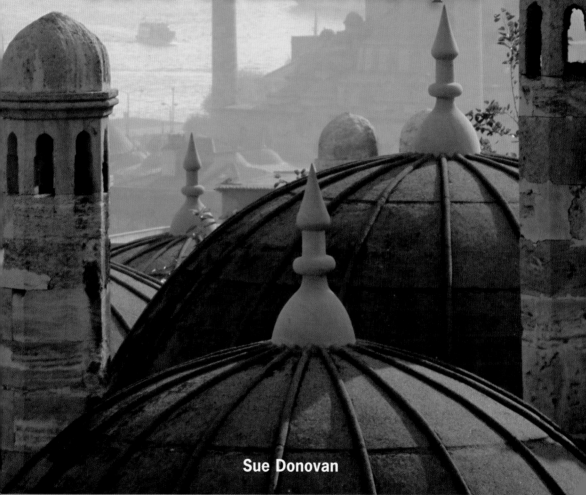

Sue Donovan

children's press®

An imprint of Scholastic Inc.

NEW YORK • TORONTO • LONDON • AUCKLAND • SYDNEY
MEXICO CITY • NEW DELHI • HONG KONG
DANBURY, CONNECTICUT

Library of Congress Cataloging-in-Publication Data

Donovan, Sue.
   Istanbul, once Constantinople / by Sue Donovan.
     p. cm. -- (Shockwave)
   Includes index.
   ISBN-10: 0-531-17755-6 (lib. bdg.)
   ISBN-13: 978-0-531-17755-6 (lib. bdg.)
   ISBN-10: 0-531-15490-4 (pbk.)
   ISBN-13: 978-0-531-15490-8 (pbk.)
 1. Istanbul (Turkey)--History--Juvenile literature. I. Title. II. Series.

   DR728.D66 2008
   949.61'8--dc22

2007022122

Published in 2008 by Children's Press, an imprint of Scholastic Inc.,
557 Broadway, New York, New York 10012
www.scholastic.com

SCHOLASTIC, CHILDREN'S PRESS, and associated logos are trademarks
and/or registered trademarks of Scholastic Inc.

08 09 10 11 12 13 14 15 16 17
10 9 8 7 6 5 4 3 2 1

Printed in China through Colorcraft Ltd., Hong Kong

Author: Sue Donovan
Educational Consultant: Ian Morrison
Editors: Avelyn Davidson and Nadja Embacher
Designer: Juliet Hughes
Photo Researcher: Jamshed Mistry
Illustration: John Bennett (p. 22)

Photographs by: Circa Art/PicturesNow.com (map, p. 8); **Getty Images** (p. 1; pp. 6–7; Hagia
Sophia, p. 13; Süleymaiye Mosque, p. 21; muezzin, street scene, pp. 24–25; carpet shop, p. 26);
Images and Stories/www.imagesandstories.com: Bahadir Taskin (robe, caftan, p. 19); **Izzet
Keribar** (women in headscarves, p. 25); **Hagia Sophia Museum Istanbul Turkey** (Constantinople,
p. 9); **Matrakci Nasuh 1543, Topkapi Palace Museum** (Süleyman's musicians, p. 20); **Jennifer and
Brian Lupton** (teenagers, pp. 30–31); **More Images/Northwind** (p. 17); **Photolibrary** (p. 5; harbour
chain, p. 9; Constantine I, p. 10; p. 12; Valens Aqueduct, p. 13; pp. 15–16; people dining out,
p. 25; walking tour, grand bazaar, Turkish sweet tea, p. 26; Spice Bazaar, Galata Bridge, p. 27;
Blue Mosque, p. 28; Basilica Cistern, Topkapi Palace, Spoonmaker's Diamond, p. 29; ship,
pp. 30–31); **Stock Central: age fotostock/Adalberto Ríos Lanz** (interior Hagia Sophia, p. 28);
topfoto/Werner Forman (Mehmet II, p. 18); **Tranz/Corbis** (cover; spires of Hagia Sophia, p. 8;
p. 11; Constantinople cross, p. 14; Topkapi Palace rooftops, Sultan's chamber, pp. 18–19;
Süleyman I, p. 20; Mehmet VI, p. 22; p. 23; doner kebab chef, p. 27; Hippodrome, p. 28; Turkish
bath, p. 29)

All other illustrations and photographs © Weldon Owen Education Inc.

CONTENTS

Christian (*KRISS chun*) a person who believes in the teachings of Jesus

conquer (*KON kur*) to take control of a place and its people

continent one of the seven main land masses on the earth

Crusader (*Kru SAY der*) one of the European Christian knights who, between 1096 and 1270, fought to recapture the Holy Land (Palestine) from the Muslims

Muslim (*MUZ lim*) a person who believes in the teachings of the Prophet Muhammad (570–632 A.D.)

secular (*SEH kyoo lur*) not connected with religion. Turkey is a secular Muslim country.

strategic (*struh TEE juhk*) **position** location with advantages due to its geographical placement

. . . .

For easy reference, see Wordmark on back flap.
For additional vocabulary, see Glossary on page 32.

The word *strategic* (an adjective) is related to the word *strategy* (a noun). Other related words include: *strategize* (a verb) and *strategically* (an adverb).

European Crusaders on their way
to the Holy Land

Istanbul (*ISS tan buhl*) has had many names. Admirers have called it "Queen of Cities," and "City of the World's Desire." For hundreds of years, it was known as Constantinople. Travelers and traders have gone there over the centuries to marvel at the city. For more than 2,500 years, it has been one of the most important cities of the world. Set in a **strategic position**, between two **continents**, it lies partly in Europe and partly in Asia. Once the capital of the Eastern Roman Empire, it was the center of the entire **Christian** world. Later, it became the capital of the **Muslim** world.

Istanbul's architecture and sites reflect the complicated mix of cultures that has taken place there. It is a city of two worlds – Eastern and Western, traditional and modern.

Asian shore

EUROPE

Black Sea

Bosporus

Golden Horn

Istanbul

ASIA

Sea of Marmara

BULGARIA
EUROPE
GREECE

Black Sea

Istanbul

Sea of Marmara

GEORGIA
ARMENIA
AZERBAIJAN

ASIA

Ankara

TURKEY

IRAN

Mediterranean Sea

SYRIA

IRAQ

CYPRUS

Two of the world's longest suspension bridges
connect Europe and Asia across the Bosporus.
One of them, the Fatih Sultan Mehmet Bridge,
or Bosporus II, is seen here. It spans 3,576 feet.

European shore

Facing the Land of the Blind

The city we call Istanbul has had a long and turbulent history. It was founded on the seven hills of a **peninsula**. The peninsula was surrounded on three sides by water – the Sea of Marmara, the **Bosporus**, and an **inlet** of the Bosporus called the Golden Horn.

Istanbul

I was uncertain about the meaning of *turbulent*. I remember a movie in which an airplane pilot warned of possible *turbulence*. I guess it means *bumpy* or *unstable*. Connections like this help make reading clearer and more interesting.

Legend has it that in 657 B.C. a Greek leader named Byzas tried to find a new home for his tribe. A **soothsayer** told him to settle at a place that faced "the land of the blind." Byzas and his people sailed up the Bosporus. There they saw people living on the Asian shore. They thought that these people must have been blind not to live around the Golden Horn. Byzas and his tribe settled on the European shore. They called their new home Byzantium.

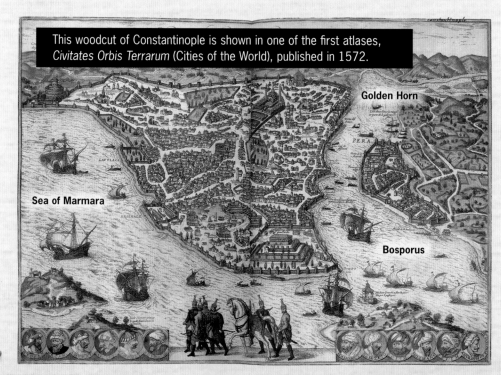

This woodcut of Constantinople is shown in one of the first atlases, *Civitates Orbis Terrarum* (Cities of the World), published in 1572.

Golden Horn

Sea of Marmara

Bosporus

This picture of the city shows the iron chain used to protect the harbor of the Golden Horn from attackers.

The chain is displayed in the Military Museum, Istanbul.

From the eighth century onward, the Byzantines protected their harbor by installing an iron chain across the entrance to the Golden Horn.

Over the course of hundreds of years, Byzantium became a rich and powerful city. On the main trade route between Europe and Asia, it was a busy seaport and center for trade. Merchants had to pay taxes on all their goods that passed through the city by either land or sea.

The New Rome

Constantine I (275–337 A.D.)

For hundreds of years, the city of Byzantium was ruled by Greeks. In about 100 B.C., it became part of the Roman Empire. By 325 A.D., the Roman Empire had grown so large that Rome was no longer at its center. The empire's wealth and learning had moved eastward to cities such as Alexandria in Egypt. Emperor Constantine I realized the difficulty of ruling the vast Roman Empire from Rome. He recognized the advantages of Byzantium's location at the crossroads of the major land and sea routes between Europe and Asia.

In 330 A.D., the city was officially made the capital of the Roman Empire. At first, the city was called New Rome. Within a few years, it was renamed Constantinople, in honor of Constantine.

The City and Its Empires (657 B.C. to 1453 A.D.)

657 B.C.
This is the legendary date for the founding of Byzantium.

330 A.D.
Byzantium becomes the capital of the Roman Empire. Its name is changed to Constantinople.

395 A.D.
The Roman Empire is split into the Western and Eastern Roman Empires.

476 A.D.
The Western Roman Empire collapses.

1204 A.D.
The Crusaders attack Constantinople.

1453 A.D.
The Ottomans capture Constantinople. The Eastern Roman Empire ends.

AUSTRIA

DACIA (now ROMANIA)

Black Sea

GALLIA (now FRANCE)

ITALIA (now ITALY)

ASIA

Byzantium or Constantinople

EUROPE

IBERIA (now SPAIN)

Rome

ASIA MINOR (now TURKEY)

ACHAEA (now GREECE)

SYR

CYPRUS

Ionian Sea

Aegean Sea

Mediterranean Sea

Alexandria

AEGYPTUS (now EGYPT)

AFRICA

Map of the Roman Empire in 395 A.D.

Istanbul, as seen here today, has twice been the capital of an empire. From 330 A.D. to 1453 A.D., it was the capital of the Eastern Roman, or Byzantine, Empire. The Ottomans also chose it as the capital of their empire from 1453 to 1922.

Constantine I was the first Christian emperor. By 392 A.D., Christianity was the official religion of the Roman Empire. Churches were being built all around the city. For the next 1,000 years, Constantinople would be the capital of the Eastern Roman Empire, later also called the Byzantine Empire. It gained enormous wealth and both economic and religious power.

An Ideal Capital
- Roman Empire had grown too large
- wealth and learning were moving east
- Byzantium was crossroads of land and sea routes
- city was well protected

The Golden Age

Justinian I (483–565 A.D.)

Constantinople was attacked many times because of its growing wealth and power. Emperor Theodosius II (401–450 A.D.) built two parallel walls around the city to protect it. There was a deep ditch on the outside, which could be filled with water. Many important structures were built at this time. They included **aqueducts** and **cisterns** to provide the city with fresh water. The city's first university was established while Theodosius was emperor.

The most famous of all the Byzantine buildings was the Hagia Sophia (*EYE uh So FEE uh*), the **Church** of Holy Wisdom. This church was built by Emperor Justinian I around 530 A.D. Next to Constantine I, Justinian was the greatest of the Byzantine emperors. His wife, Theodora, was a beautiful and intelligent woman. She had great influence on political affairs. This was unusual. Women rarely held political power in those days.

Theodora (508–548 A.D.) was Justinian's wife and adviser. This Byzantine **mosaic** shows her with two men and seven women assisting her.

I don't know the correct pronunciation of *Theodosius*, but I guess, whichever way I say it, the meaning will remain the same. Not worrying too much about pronunciation helps me to read more fluently.

SHOCKER

During Istanbul's long history, 60 fires and 50 major earthquakes have caused great destruction. In 542 A.D., 60 percent of the population were killed by a deadly disease called plague.

Two Byzantine structures, the Hagia Sophia (above) and the Valens Aqueduct (below), still stand today.

West Meets East

Christian cross

For hundreds of years, Constantinople was defended successfully against its attackers. But within the city walls, the throne changed hands often. In 1195, Emperor Isaac II was overthrown by his brother. Isaac's son Alexius traveled to Europe to find help for his father. Alexius promised money to the **Crusaders** if they helped restore his father to the throne. The Crusaders needed money for their plan to take the city of Jerusalem back from the Muslims. They agreed to help Alexius.

In 1203, the Crusaders **conquered** Constantinople. Isaac was too ill to be emperor, so his son Alexius IV ruled. Alexius couldn't pay the Crusaders because he had run out of money. He wanted to tax the people, but they refused. The people of Constantinople blamed him for the Crusaders' brutal attack on the city. They killed Alexius IV. A new emperor, Alexius V, came to the throne.

The Crusaders were still waiting for payment. Their army **besieged** the city for many months. Finally, in 1204, the Crusaders broke through the walls of the city. For three days, they looted all of the city's treasures. They killed men, women, and children. The Christian armies of the West almost destroyed the great Christian city of the East.

The word *crusade* comes from the Latin word *crux*, meaning "cross." The cross is a symbol of Christianity.

The Capture of Constantinople in 1204 by sixteenth-century Italian painter Jacopo Robusti Tintoretto

15

A Great Victory

Mehmet II (1432–1481)

After 1204, the Byzantine Empire gradually became weaker. At the same time, a new empire was becoming powerful. A group of Turkish Muslims, called the Ottomans, was advancing from the East. By 1350, they had captured all the lands on the Asian shore around Constantinople. Over the next hundred years, the Ottomans attacked Constantinople several times, but they were not able to break through the thousand-year-old walls. Constantinople, the city ruled by Christians, was now surrounded by lands ruled by the Muslim Ottomans.

In 1452, the Ottoman **sultan** Mehmet II set out to win the great prize – Constantinople. The city's emperor, Constantine XI, had only 26 ships and 7,000 men. Mehmet had 70 ships and an army of 100,000 men. He realized that he needed to attack the Golden Horn. The great iron chain that blocked the harbor presented a problem for the attackers. Mehmet solved that problem by building a road over a 200-foot hill. His ships were dragged over the hill and lowered into the Golden Horn. Mehmet also had a secret weapon – a massive cannon. He used 30 pairs of oxen to drag the cannon to the city's walls. For about two months, Mehmet's cannon bombarded the city walls.

Finally, Mehmet's army broke through the famous walls and marched into the city. The Byzantines prayed and rang their church bells. But nothing could save them. The **siege** was over, and the Byzantine Empire was dead. In 1453, Mehmet II finally became the Sultan of Constantinople, the new capital of the expanding Ottoman Empire.

Mehmet II   vs.   **Constantine XI**

- 70 ships
- 100,000 men
- cannon

- 26 ships
- 7,000 men
- strong defenses

Mehmet II won after a long siege.

The victorious Sultan Mehmet II enters the captured city in 1453.

SHOCKER

The Byzantines had a secret weapon – Greek fire. This was a **flammable** mixture they threw or sprayed on their enemies. Not even water could put it out! The exact recipe was so secret that it remains unknown today.

Rebirth of the City

Mehmet II was only twenty-one when he conquered Constantinople. He built himself a palace in the best position in Istanbul. He called it Topkapi *(Top KAH pee)*, which means "gate of the cannon." Topkapi was the home of the sultans and the heart of the Ottoman Empire. All the important tasks of government took place there.

Mehmet the Conqueror

After the siege, most of the Byzantine Greeks fled from the city. To repopulate the city, Mehmet encouraged their return. He also brought in thousands of Muslim and Jewish people. Most churches were turned into **mosques**, but Mehmet gave everyone the freedom to practice their religion. For many centuries, the different religious groups lived peacefully side by side. The heads of the various religions were responsible to the sultan for the behavior of their people.

The heading indicates that this page will be about how the city changed after it was conquered. Predicting what will be discussed gives a good context for reading on.

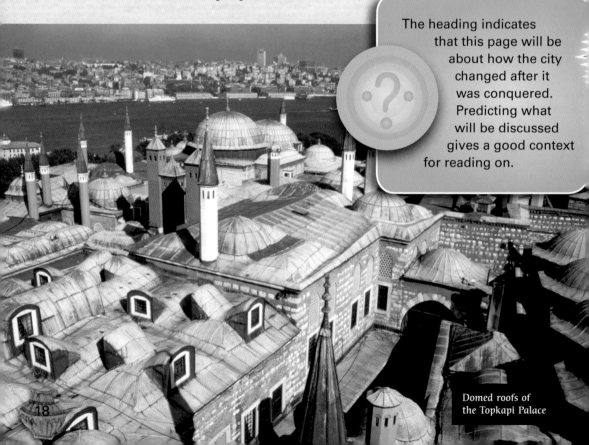

Domed roofs of the Topkapi Palace

The sultan's chamber in the harem

The Topkapi Palace

At the Topkapi Palace, the word of the sultan was law. The only tower in the palace was called the Tower of Justice because court decisions for the city were made there. It was also a watchtower for the city and the entrance to the **harem**. The harem was the private living quarters of the sultan's wives and family. The harem was ruled by the sultan's mother. There was constant gossip and rivalry as women in the harem vied to become the sultan's favorite. The sultan's many children were also rivals. Sometimes sons were locked away so that they could not plot against their father. After a sultan died, his entire harem would be moved to another palace.

The dagger (above) and the caftan (below) are two **artifacts** from the time of the sultans that can be seen at the Topkapi Museum today.

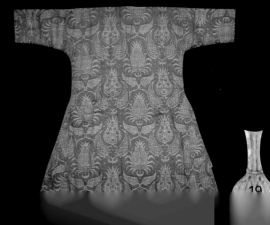

The Ottoman Empire

After Mehmet II, one of the most important sultans was Süleyman I, also known as Süleyman the Magnificent. He became sultan in 1520.

Süleyman I (1495–1566)

In the **Islamic** world, he was named "The Lawgiver," because he reformed the Ottoman legal system. Süleyman was famous for conquering many lands. He personally led his army as far as Austria. During his long reign, he doubled the size of the Ottoman Empire.

Süleyman I was a man of great learning. He loved poetry and art. Süleyman employed a clever architect named Sinan. Hundreds of buildings, such as mosques, schools, bridges, and palaces, were designed by Sinan.

Under Ottoman rule, the city was known as Istanbul. It expanded and changed. Many fine mosques were built that are still part of Istanbul's splendor today.

This picture, which is now in the Topkapi Museum, shows musicians entertaining Süleyman the Magnificent.

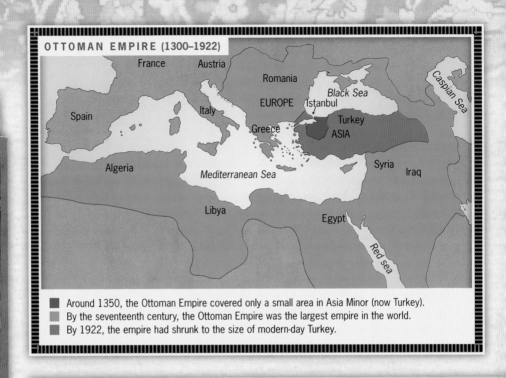

OTTOMAN EMPIRE (1300–1922)

France
Austria
Romania
Black Sea
Spain
Italy
EUROPE
Istanbul
Turkey
ASIA
Greece
Caspian Sea
Algeria
Mediterranean Sea
Syria
Iraq
Libya
Egypt
Red sea

■ Around 1350, the Ottoman Empire covered only a small area in Asia Minor (now Turkey).
■ By the seventeenth century, the Ottoman Empire was the largest empire in the world.
■ By 1922, the empire had shrunk to the size of modern-day Turkey.

The Süleymaniye Mosque

The Süleymaniye Mosque was designed by Sinan during Süleyman's reign. It took only seven years to build. Churches of similar size built in Europe at that time sometimes took hundreds of years to complete.

The Birth of Modern Turkey

By 1900, the Ottoman Empire was shrinking. The sultans were losing their power. Leaders in the army wanted to modernize the empire. They had formed a government and now ruled the country. To regain the territory they had lost, they decided to fight on the side of Germany in World War I (1914–1918).

Mehmet VI (1861–1926)

After Germany lost the war, the Ottoman Empire collapsed. Turkey was occupied by foreign armies, including the Greeks. A brilliant young army officer, Mustafa Kemal, became the leader of the Turkish independence movement. He led the Turkish people in a War of Independence (1919–1923). In 1922, he defeated the Greek army. All other foreign armies that had occupied Turkey since the end of World War I also agreed to leave. The last sultan, Mehmet VI, turned over power to Mustafa Kemal and his nationalist movement.

One year later, a peace treaty was signed in Lausanne, Switzerland, with Greece and other countries. Under the Treaty of Lausanne, Turkey was recognized internationally as an independent state. Turkey became a republic. Ankara was its new capital. Mustafa Kemal was elected president. He became known as Atatürk, Father of the Turks. His government made many changes to turn Turkey into a modern nation.

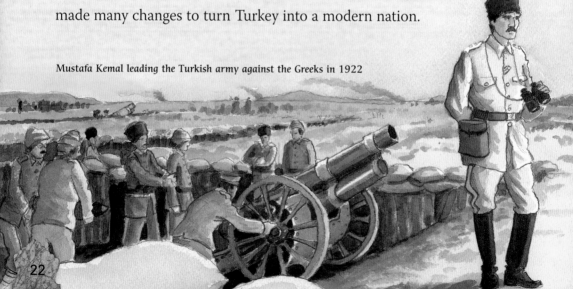

Mustafa Kemal leading the Turkish army against the Greeks in 1922

The Great Reformer

Here are some of the reforms Atatürk introduced to Turkey. Not all of them were popular at the time.

- He introduced the Western alphabet in place of Arabic.
- He made surnames compulsory.
- He separated religion from government.
- He helped women gain the right to vote.
- He outlawed the wearing of the fez, a traditional headwear for men.

Turkey's Road to Independence

- fought on Germany's side during World War I
  ↓
- Germany lost – Ottoman Empire collapsed
  ↓
- Turkey occupied by foreign armies
  ↓
- Mustafa Kemal defeated Greek occupiers
  ↓
- all foreign armies left
  ↓
- Turkey became an independent state

One City, Many Worlds

Muezzin calling from minaret

In 1930, Atatürk officially changed the city's name from Constantinople to Istanbul. Although Ankara is now the capital, Istanbul is still Turkey's biggest and most important city. About ten million people live there. It remains Turkey's commercial and cultural center.

Istanbul is still a city of contrasts. You will see many people wearing the latest fashions and some who are dressed more traditionally. Some people drive expensive cars, while others cannot afford to pay the bus fare. Young people enjoy Western-style fast food, but they also eat traditional food, such as *simit*. A simit is a circular bread with sesame seeds that has been eaten by Turks for hundreds of years.

Everywhere you will find young men and women in Internet cafes. Next to them, you will see men playing backgammon and drinking the traditional strong Turkish coffee. As you walk along, you will hear the lively music of Turkish pop bands. Five times a day, you will hear loud singing from the **minarets** of mosques. The Muslims among the population are being called to prayer by the **muezzin**.

Istanbul is a melting pot of different ethnic backgrounds, religions, and languages. During the last 2,500 years, these elements have combined to create a city of great architectural beauty with a unique history and culture.

Simit is like a Turkish bagel. Bagels are popular throughout the world, and different countries have some unusual names for them:
Austria – *beugel*
China – *girde nan*
Lithuania – *riestainiai*
Russia – *bublik*

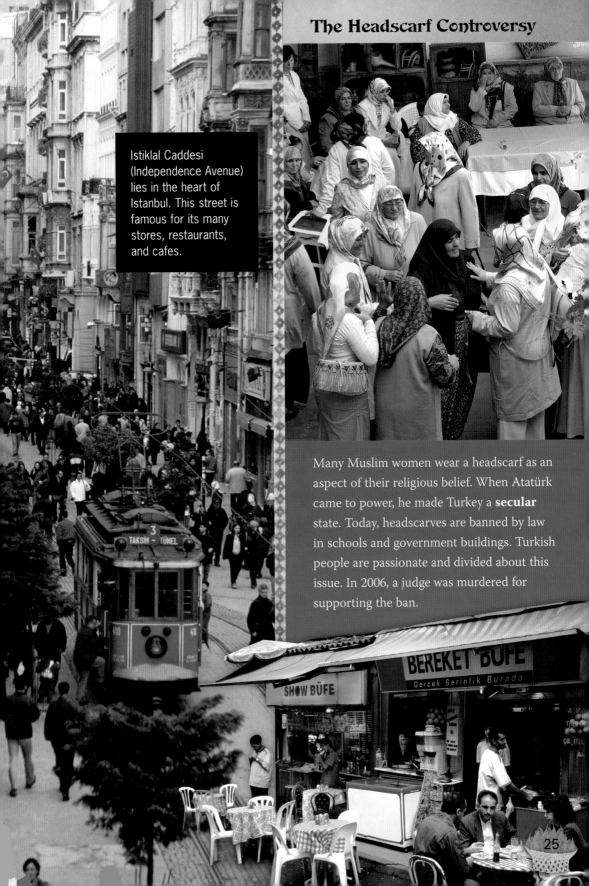

The Headscarf Controversy

Istiklal Caddesi (Independence Avenue) lies in the heart of Istanbul. This street is famous for its many stores, restaurants, and cafes.

Many Muslim women wear a headscarf as an aspect of their religious belief. When Atatürk came to power, he made Turkey a **secular** state. Today, headscarves are banned by law in schools and government buildings. Turkish people are passionate and divided about this issue. In 2006, a judge was murdered for supporting the ban.

A Walking Tour of Istanbul

One of the best ways to see Istanbul is to take a walking tour. We join a guided tour that takes us around the city.

First we go to the Grand **Bazaar**. It is very old and HUGE! There are more than 4,000 shops full of carpets, jewelry, and tourists!

shopkeepers bring us sweet tea in little glasses and beg to show us their wares. Our guide tells us how to bargain:

1. Don't show enthusiasm.
2. Let the merchant give a price first.
3. Don't be afraid to walk away, and maybe come back.

We buy only a few small souvenirs, because we don't want to carry a carpet around all day!

We walk downhill to the Spice Bazaar. It is full of brightly colored spices, dried fruit, and honey. It smells wonderful. Best of all is the Turkish delight – a jelly-like candy coated with powdered sugar.

Next stop is the Galata Bridge across the Bosporus. We climb up some steep, winding streets to the Galata Tower. The 360-degree view from the balcony at the top is fantastic.

This Turkish speciality is called doner kebab. It is slices of lamb wrapped in flat bread. After that delicious lunch, we stroll on to the Hippodrome.

The Hippodrome was an enormous ancient stadium. It was completed by Constantine in 330 B.C. It was built for horse-racing events. It held up to 60,000 spectators. Today, only the tall **obelisks** that stood in the middle of the stadium remain. The side walls are completely gone. The Ottomans used the stones for building material.

The Blue Mosque is next to the Hippodrome. Its domed roof and its six minarets are visible from many parts of the city. It is called "Blue" because of the blue tiles inside. Before entering, people must remove their shoes, as the mosque is still used as a place of worship.

Some people say the Hagia Sophia is the eighth Wonder of the World. Its huge domed ceiling is 182 feet high and 102 feet wide. There are thousands of brilliant mosaics. They picture religious scenes and Byzantine emperors from when it was used as a Christian church. The Ottomans turned this church into a mosque. In 1935, Atatürk turned it into a museum. Now the magnificent Hagia Sophia can be admired by everyone. We lose track of time as we gaze at this breathtaking place.

A must-see in Istanbul is the Basilica Cistern. It was built in the sixth century to supply water for the palaces nearby. It can hold 2,800,000 cubic feet of water. We go down 52 stone steps to a spooky underground chamber.

The Topkapi Palace holds the remaining treasures of the Ottoman Empire. As we stroll around the palace and grounds, we are immersed in history. In the harem, we see the 40 rooms that belonged to the sultan's mother. The treasury is full of magnificent artifacts. The priceless Spoonmaker's Diamond, one of the world's biggest diamonds, is the most dazzling of all.

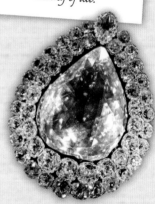

The Spoonmaker's Diamond is pear-shaped. It is set among 49 smaller diamonds.

Our last stop for the day is at a Turkish bath, or hammam. Turkish baths go back to the time of the Romans. The hammam we go to was built in 1557. There are separate baths for men and women. We sit on a hot stone slab. It is very steamy. It is just the right thing after walking and gazing around all day. What a refreshing way to end our tour of Istanbul!

Throughout its long history, Istanbul has experienced many disasters, including destructive fires and earthquakes. But the biggest threat of all comes from pollution. Each year, more than 50,000 ships pass through the Bosporus. Many are carrying oil and natural gas from the Black Sea area of Russia.

WHAT DO YOU THINK?

Given Istanbul's historic significance and large population, should tankers be allowed to travel through the Bosporus?

PRO

There have always been disasters on the Bosporus. But trade and shipping cannot be banned. They are too important for the people living in and around the city. The risk of oil spills can be reduced by making the tankers smaller and safer.

Collisions sometimes happen because the strait is busy and very narrow. Huge amounts of oil can be spilled. This causes grave environmental problems. The oil spills can endanger the health of the animals living in the Bosporus and the people and animals living alongside it.

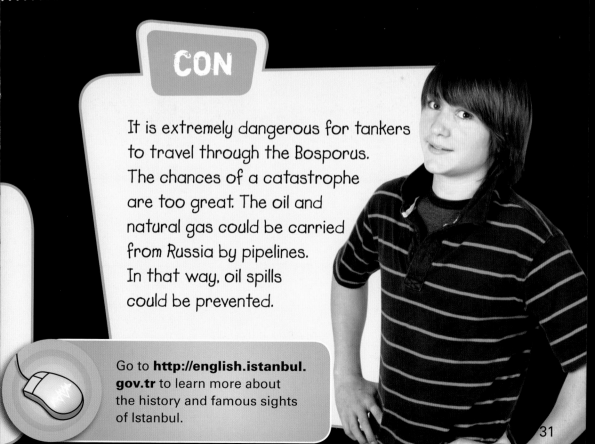

CON

It is extremely dangerous for tankers to travel through the Bosporus. The chances of a catastrophe are too great. The oil and natural gas could be carried from Russia by pipelines. In that way, oil spills could be prevented.

Go to **http://english.istanbul. gov.tr** to learn more about the history and famous sights of Istanbul.

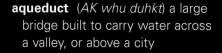

GLOSSARY

aqueduct (*AK whu duhkt*) a large bridge built to carry water across a valley, or above a city

artifact (*ART uh fakt*) an object used in the past

bazaar (*buh ZAR*) a street market or a covered market in the Middle East with rows of shops

besiege (*buh SEEJ*) to surround a city, cut off supplies, and wait for people inside to surrender

Bosporus (*BOSS puh ruhss*) a strait between European and Asian Turkey

church a building used by Christians for worship

cistern (*SISS turn*) a reservoir or tank for storing water

flammable (*FLAM uh buhl*) likely to catch fire

harem (*HAIR uhm*) a separate house or part of a house for the women of a Muslim household

inlet a narrow body of water that leads inland from an ocean

Islam (*ISS lahm*) the religion based on the teachings of Muhammad. Muslims believe that Allah is God and Muhammad is his prophet.

minaret (*min u RET*) the tall, thin tower of a mosque, from which Muslims are called to prayer

mosaic (*moh ZAY ik*) a pattern or picture made up of small pieces of colored stone, tile, or glass

mosque (*MOSK*) a building used by Muslims for worship

muezzin (*mu EH tzin*) a Muslim crier who calls the hour of daily prayers

obelisk (*AHB uh lisk*) an upright stone pillar with a top shaped like a pyramid

peninsula (*puh NIN suh luh*) a long, thin piece of land almost surrounded by water

siege (*SEEJ*) a long, drawn-out attack on a city or town

soothsayer a person who supposedly predicts the future

sultan (*SUHL tuhn*) an emperor or ruler of some Muslim countries

INDEX